Old-School Love: New-School Parenting with Old-School Flavor

Old-School Love: New-School Parenting with Old-School Flavor

Published By Dr. Solomon Armstead Pittsburgh, PA

ISBN 979-8-218-29267-6

This Book is Dedicated to my Mama

Table of Contents

Welcome to the parenting workbook that will help you rediscover the wisdom of old-school thinking and apply it to your modern challenges. You might think that old-school parenting is outdated, rigid, or even harsh, but that's not true. Old-school parenting is based on morals and values that still matter today, such as respect, responsibility, honesty, and kindness. Old school parents also knew how to show love and affection in ways that nurtured their children's growth and development. They didn't need fancy gadgets, expensive toys, or elaborate activities to bond with their kids. They used simple but powerful tools like family dinners, listening sessions, singing songs, and sitting on the front porch or stoop. These practices created rich and robust levels of engagement that helped children feel secure, confident, and happy. Of course, old-school parenting doesn't mean ignoring the new-school parenting concepts that have emerged from research and experience. It means finding a balance between the best of both worlds. For example, old-school parents might not have known about the benefits of positive reinforcement, but they did praise their children for their efforts and achievements. New school parents might not have experienced the hardships of the past, but they do face new challenges such as cyberbullying, screen addiction, and social media pressure. By combining old-school values with new-school strategies, you can create a parenting style that works for you and your child.

In this workbook, you will learn how to apply old-school love to your parenting challenges. You will discover how old-school love has been and is the bedrock for our children and future generations. You will also find practical tips, exercises, and activities that will help you strengthen your parent-child relationship and raise happy, healthy, and successful kids. So grab a pen, a paper, and a cup of coffee (or tea), and get ready to embark on an exciting journey of old school love!

Solomon Armstrong

THOUGHT PARTNERS

I was riding in a jitney when we stopped to get gas. A young woman walked in front of the car and my eyes followed her all the way to her car. When I looked up to see why my jitney hadn't got out of the car yet, I realized he was watching me, while I was watching her. He interrupted my study session and asked, "You plan on going over there?" "Nope." I meant it. "Nothing wrong with looking", I said. "Then don't look where you don't want to go", he said smiling. I had just got done telling him I was in a relationship that I wanted to make work. He took the time to teach me something valuable that I never considered. He concluded "it takes years to build trust and only seconds to lose it. It was the smooth challenge to my thinking and warning that I needed. My jitney was my first thought partner.

Thought partners are people who can provide intellectual, emotional, and practical support to individuals, including parents, helping them cope with the challenges of raising children. Thought partners can be friends, relatives, co-workers, mentors, or anyone who shares a common interest or goal with the single parent. Research and studies have shown that thought partners can benefit single parents in various ways, such as:

- **Reducing stress and improving mental health.** Parents often face high levels of stress, anxiety, and depression due to the multiple demands/responsibilities they must juggle.

Thought partners can offer a listening ear, a shoulder to lean on, and a sounding board for ideas and solutions. They can also provide positive feedback, encouragement, and affirmation that can boost the parent's self-esteem and confidence.

- **Enhancing parenting skills and child outcomes.** Parents may struggle with parenting issues such as discipline, communication, education, and socialization. Thought partners can offer advice, guidance, and resources that can help single parents improve their parenting skills and practices. They can also serve as role models and mentors for the children, providing them with additional support, care, and opportunities. Studies have found that children of single parents who have strong social networks tend to have better academic performance, behavior, and well-being than those who lack such support.

Reflect on how you rid your mind of "shoulda/coulda/woulda "thoughts that only keep you stuck.

- **Expanding social capital and economic opportunities.** Single parents may face isolation, discrimination, and limited access to resources and opportunities due to their family status. Thought partners can help single parents expand their social capital by introducing them to new people, groups, and organizations that can offer them valuable information, connections, and assistance. They can also help single parents explore and pursue economic opportunities such as education, training, employment, entrepreneurship, or financial aid that can improve their income and stability.

Who have you identified as a potential thought partner? What is their knowledge or skill that directly benefits you and/or your child?

_____
_____
_____
_____
_____
_____
_____
_____
_____

Based on your personal experience, which of them helped you boost your confidence in friends?

_____
_____
_____
_____
_____
_____
_____
_____
_____

What to pay attention to:

Watch your emotional posture. Accountability is not meant to hurt you. When no offense is meant, no offense should be given. Let it go so you can grow.

Consider this:

It is important for individuals to identify potential thought partners in their lives and strengthen their relationships with them. Some tips on how to do this are:
- **Be proactive and intentional.** Seek out people who share your values, interests, goals, or challenges. Reach out to them regularly and express your interest in learning from them and supporting them.
- **Be open and honest.** Share your thoughts, feelings, needs, and expectations with your thought partners. Listen to their feedback and respect their opinions. Be willing to accept constructive criticism.
- **Be reciprocal and appreciative.** Offer your thought partners your time, attention, expertise, and resources. Help them with their problems and celebrate their successes. Express your gratitude and appreciation for their contribution to your life.
- **Be respectful and trustworthy.** Honor your commitments and agreements with your thought partners. Keep your promises and respect their boundaries. Protect their privacy and confidentiality.
It's important to note that the effectiveness of thought partners may vary depending on the individual circumstances of each parent and their unique needs and challenges.

PURPOSE AND MEANING

One of the saddest things I witnessed while working with families entangled in the system was when families were asked what their strengths were, they had no answer. Feeling a mix of compassion and sorrow I would often render some suggestions. Largely this stems from parents who were reared in families that didn't challenge them to identify their own purpose.

Purpose and meaning can be defined as a long-term goal that is meaningful to the self and intended to contribute to the world beyond the self. Purpose and meaning can guide life decisions, influence behavior, shape goals, offer a sense of direction, and create meaning. For some people, purpose and meaning are connected to their vocation, such as developing futuristic ideas or providing the best life for their family. For others, purpose and meaning are related to their spirituality, values, or passions.

One of the domains where purpose and meaning can have a profound impact is family life. Family purpose is a long-term goal that families share across generations and that becomes meaningful to younger family members as they form their own plans to accomplish acts of consequence to the world beyond themselves. Family purposes can foster moral development, social responsibility, and intergenerational solidarity among family members. Family purpose can also help families cope with challenges, overcome adversity, and thrive in changing times. However, not all families have a clear or shared sense of purpose. Some families may struggle to identify their own strengths, values, or goals.

Some families may face difficulties in communicating, collaborating, or supporting each other. Some families may experience conflicts, stress, or trauma that undermine their cohesion and well-being. These factors can affect the quality of family relationships and the development of children. Research has shown that a lack of purpose and meaning in family life can have negative consequences for child-rearing. For example, parents who lack purpose and meaning may have lower levels of parental satisfaction, involvement, warmth, and responsiveness. and suicidal ideation. They may also have higher levels of parental stress, depression, anxiety, and burnout. Children who grow up in families without purpose and meaning may have lower levels of self-esteem, self-regulation, academic achievement, and prosocial behavior. They may also have higher levels of emotional problems, behavioral problems, substance abuse, therefore, it is crucial for families to find and cultivate their purpose and meaning in life.

"By loving them for more than their abilities, we show our children that they are much more than the sum of their accomplishments."

-Eileen Kennedy-Moor

There are several ways that families can do this. One way is to engage in activities that reflect their values and interests as a family unit. For example, families can volunteer for a social cause, participate in a religious community, or pursue a hobby together. Another way is to have regular conversations about their goals, dreams, hopes, and fears as a family unit. For example, families can share their stories, express their feelings, listen to each other's perspectives, and provide feedback and encouragement. A third way is to seek professional help if they encounter challenges or obstacles that prevent them from finding or fulfilling their purpose and meaning as a family unit. For example, families can consult with counselors, therapists, coaches, or mentors who can offer guidance and support.

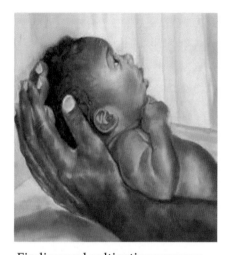

Finding and cultivating purpose and meaning in family life can have positive outcomes for child-rearing. Research has shown that parents who have purpose and meaning tend to have higher levels of parental satisfaction, involvement, warmth, and responsiveness. They also tend to have lower levels of parental stress, depression, anxiety, and burnout. Children who grow up in families with purpose and meaning tend to have higher levels of self-esteem, self-regulation, academic achievement, and prosocial behavior. They also tend to have lower levels of emotional problems, behavioral problems, substance abuse, and suicidal ideation. By seeking professional help, families can foster moral development, social responsibility, and intergenerational solidarity among family members. They can also cope with challenges, overcome adversity, and thrive in changing times.

What are the strengths of your family?

_____
_____
_____
_____
_____
_____
_____
_____
_____

What is your role or purpose as it relates to your family?

_____
_____
_____
_____
_____
_____
_____
_____
_____

What to pay attention to:

"Loneliness can be a signal that your connections with others are fading." It is a path that leads to depression. Don't stay there long. It may not be your thing but reach out to your friends first. Meet up. And if at a possible don't leave their presence without a deep loving embrace.

Take a moment to reflect on the healthiest version of your family that you can envision. How can you bridge where you are to where you would like to be?

DIFFICULT CONVERSATIONS

Being a single parent is not easy. You have to juggle many responsibilities and face many challenges, such as providing for your family, managing your household, and raising your child. Sometimes, you may feel overwhelmed and stressed out by the demands of your situation. You may also feel lonely and isolated, especially if you lack social support or face stigma from others.

How can you have difficult conversations with your child when you are struggling with these issues? One of the most important things you can do is to build a strong and positive relationship with your child. According to Kenneth Barish, Ph.D., a clinical associate professor of psychology at Weill Medical College, Cornell University, and author of Pride and Joy: A Guide to Understanding Your Child's Emotions and Solving Family Problems, this means expressing enthusiastic interest in your child's interests, acknowledging their frustrations, disappointments, and grievances, and sharing personal stories. These strategies are a great framework that can help you engage your child in dialogue with less defensiveness and less argument.

Many of these things "Big-Momma-Nem" did not model for us which is why we must begin to rewrite the narrative by employing a new set of parenting techniques.

Expressing eager interest in your child's interests means showing genuine curiosity and appreciation for what your child likes to do, whether it is sports, music, art, or anything else.

You can ask open-ended questions, listen attentively, praise their efforts, and join them in their activities. This can help your child feel valued and respected, as well as boost their self-esteem and confidence. (Avoid dry teasing or making fun of your child while showing curiosity and appreciation for what your child likes to do.)

Acknowledging their frustrations, disappointments, and grievances means validating their feelings and empathizing with their struggles. You can say things like "I know you feel it wasn't fair when...", "I know you were really disappointed when...", or "I know you were really frustrated and angry when...".

This can help your child feel understood and supported, as well as reduce their resentment and hostility. Sharing personal stories means telling your child about experiences in your own life that are relevant to what they are going through. You can tell them about how you dealt with similar problems or emotions, what you learned from them, or how you overcame them. This can help your child feel connected and inspired, as well as learn from your example. However, expressing interest, acknowledging feelings, and sharing stories may not be enough if you are facing poverty or other hardships that disrupt your efforts to communicate with your child.

Poverty can affect your mental health, physical health, social relationships, and access to resources. It can also expose your child to more stressors, such as violence, instability, discrimination, or trauma. These factors can make it harder for you to have difficult conversations with your child. Therefore, you need to be culturally competent and sensitive to the context of your situation.
Cultural competence means being aware of and respectful of the diversity and uniqueness of different cultures, backgrounds, beliefs, values, and experiences.

It also means being able to adapt your communication style and strategies to fit the needs and preferences of your child. For example, some cultures may value directness and honesty more than others; some may prefer storytelling or humor more than others; some may have different norms or expectations for parent-child relationships than others.

Being "real (honest) & relevant" can help you avoid misunderstandings or conflicts with your child that may arise from cultural differences or assumptions. It can also help you foster a sense of belonging and identity for your child that can enhance their self-esteem and resilience. You also need to find solutions and work-arounds that are healthy and helpful for both you and your child.

Assess your current reality? How does difficult conversations currently play out with your kids? Do you maintain patience and openness, understanding and emotional control? Or do you "go off"?

_____
_____
_____
_____
_____
_____
_____
_____
_____

There is always room for improvement. How can your navigation of difficult conversations improve?

_____
_____
_____
_____
_____
_____
_____
_____
_____

What to pay attention to:

Having difficult conversations with your child as a parent is not easy but it is possible. By building a strong and positive relationship with your child, being age-appropriate and sensitive to the context of your situation, and finding solutions and work-arounds that are healthy and helpful for both you and your child that can strengthen your bond, enhance your communication and promote your child's social and moral development.

Consider this:

-Seek professional help if you or your child are experiencing mental health issues such as depression, anxiety or trauma. You can look for a low-cost or free counseling service in your community or online.
-Seek social support from friends, family members, neighbors, or other single parents who can offer emotional support, practical assistance, or companionship. You can join a support group or an online forum for single parents.
-Seek financial assistance from government programs or charitable organizations that can help you with basic needs such as food, housing, healthcare, or education. You can also look for ways to increase your income or reduce your expenses.
-Seek educational opportunities for yourself or your child that can improve your skills or qualifications for better employment or career prospects. You can enroll in online courses or vocational training programs.
-Seek recreational activities for yourself or your child that can provide fun, relaxation, or enjoyment. You can find free or low-cost events or programs in your community or online.

By finding solutions and work-arounds that are healthy and helpful for both you and your child. You can improve your quality of life and well-being. You can also model positive coping skills and problem-solving skills for your child that can help them deal with their own challenges.

Bonus Article

WHAT THEY SAID, WHAT THEY MEANT, HOW IT'S SAID NOW.

1. *"I'm not one of your little friends."* **"Remember, I'm your parent first, not your friend."**

2. *"Do I look like booboo the fool?"* **"Do you think I don't understand what's going on?"**

3. *"A hard head makes a soft behind."* **"If you don't listen, you'll learn the hard way."**

4. *"You got McDonald's money?"*: **"Do you have your own money to buy that?"**

5. ***"Don't you get in trouble following behind them white kids."***: "Be careful about the influence of your peers."

6. *"I hope you know that school work like you know them songs."*: **"I hope you're putting as much effort into your studies as you do into your hobbies."**

7. ***"You smellin' yourself."***: "Don't get too full of yourself."

8. *"When we get in this store, don't touch nothin'."*: **"Please behave appropriately in public places."**

9. ***"Fix your face."***: "Adjust your attitude."

10. ***"First of all, check your tone."***: "Please speak respectfully."

11. ***"Stop all that crying before I give you something to cry about."***: "Calm down and express your feelings in a constructive way."

12. ***"Don't go out of here looking like who would have thought it"***:

13. ***"You smellin' yourself."***: "Stay humble and grounded."

14. ***"In or out."***: "Please stop letting the bugs in and the a/c out"

15. ***"You smell like outside."***: "Lets try to do a better job maintaining good hygiene."

16. ***"Blessed and highly favored"***: "I'm grateful for the good things in my life."

17. ***"It takes a strong woman to fill that cup"***: "It requires strength and resilience to fulfill one's responsibilities."

"There is no such thing as a perfect parent. So just be a real one."

~ Sue Atkins

15

WHAT THEY SAID, WHAT THEY MEANT, HOW IT'S SAID NOW. Cont'd

These interpretations aim to convey the same wisdom and life lessons in a manner that aligns with modern parenting styles and practices. These sayings reflect African American culture in several ways:

"Grandfathers are just antique little boys." ~ Unknown

1. Respect for Elders: Phrases like "I'm not one of your little friends" and "Do I look like booboo the fool?" reflect the importance placed on respect for elders in African American culture.
2. Emphasis on Education: Sayings such as "You better know that school work the same way you know those song lyrics" highlight the value placed on education.
3. Importance of Humility: Phrases like "You smellin' yourself" serve as reminders to remain humble.
4. Value of Money: The phrase "You got McDonald's money?" is a lesson about understanding the value of money.
5. Awareness of Social Realities: Sayings like "Don't you get in trouble following behind them white kids" reflect the realities of racial disparities and the need for caution.

These sayings, while they might seem confusing at first, are part of the unique language and wisdom passed down through generations. They serve as life lessons, guiding principles, and cultural preservation tools, reflecting the resilience, wisdom, and spirit of the African American community.

These cultural elements are crucial for building a strong family foundation as they foster unity, identity, and a sense of belonging. Here's how thriving families use each of these to build their lives:

1. **Storytelling:** Families use storytelling to pass down wisdom, morals, and family history. For example, grandparents might share stories about their childhood or historical events they've witnessed, which not only entertains but also educates younger generations about their heritage and the struggles their ancestors overcame.

2. **Music and Dance:** Music and dance are often central to family gatherings and celebrations. They serve as a means of expression and connection. For instance, families might have traditions around singing or dancing together at reunions or holidays, which helps strengthen bonds and create lasting memories.

WHAT THEY SAID, WHAT THEY MEANT, HOW IT'S SAID NOW. Cont'd

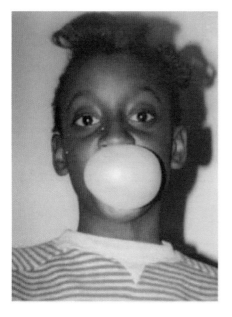

"Flattery is like chewing gum. Enjoy it but don't swallow it."

~Hank Ketcham

Take a moment to reflect on how intentional you are with your word choice and tone while talking to your kids. Are you talking to them like they are someone you love?

3. **Oral Traditions**: Oral traditions like folk tales, songs, and festivals help preserve cultural heritage. Families might have specific songs they sing together or tales they tell, which instill a sense of pride and continuity in younger generations.

4. **Food and Cuisine:** Cooking and sharing meals is a significant family activity. Families might have recipes that have been passed down through generations. Preparing these dishes together can be a bonding experience, and eating them is a way of participating in shared cultural heritage.

5. **Religious Beliefs and Practices:** Shared religious practices can provide a strong sense of community and shared values. Regular church attendance or home-based practices like prayer or Bible reading can offer comfort, guidance, and a shared moral framework.

6. **Hair and Beauty:** Hair care routines can be an important bonding experience. For example, a mother might teach her daughter how to care for her hair, passing down techniques that have been in the family for generations. This not only preserves tradition but also instills a sense of pride in one's appearance and cultural identity.

7. **Language:** Speaking African American Vernacular English (AAVE) at home can be a way of affirming cultural identity and creating a sense of belonging. It's also a way of passing down linguistic traditions to younger generations.

In all these ways, cultural traditions contribute to the strength and resilience of families, fostering unity while also celebrating unique heritage.

Section 4

DOSAGE AND INTENSITY

Applying the right dosage and intensity in child-rearing is a delicate process that requires a balance of discipline, guidance, and nurturing. Child-rearing practices vary across cultures, contexts, and families, but some universal factors that affect them are economic survival, family cohesion, and cultural transmission. In this section, I will discuss how these factors influence child-rearing in a cultural context and lens, and how the right dose can make all the difference. I will also present some strategies that can help parents and caregivers meet their children's needs at different stages of development.

Economic survival refers to the ability of families to provide for their children's basic needs, such as food, shelter, health, and education. In urban settings, economic survival can be challenging due to factors such as poverty, unemployment, low wages, high living costs, and limited access to resources and services. These factors can affect child-rearing in various ways, such as reducing parental time and attention, increasing parental stress and depression, limiting parental choices and opportunities, and exposing children to risks and hazards.

Therefore, applying the right dose of economic support and protection is crucial for child-rearing in urban contexts. This can include seeking financial assistance, accessing social services, finding affordable housing, securing stable employment, managing household budget, and investing in children's education. Family cohesion refers to the degree of closeness, harmony, and support among family members.

In urban settings, family cohesion can be influenced by factors such as migration, mobility, diversity, individualism, and social isolation. These factors can affect child-rearing in various ways, such as changing family structures and roles, disrupting family traditions and values, weakening family bonds and networks, and increasing family conflicts and violence. Therefore, applying the right dose of family involvement and communication is essential for child-rearing in urban contexts. This can include maintaining contact with extended family members, respecting cultural differences and preferences, fostering mutual understanding and respect, resolving disputes peacefully, and expressing love and affection.

Cultural transmission refers to the process of passing on cultural knowledge, beliefs, values, norms, and practices from one generation to another. In urban settings, cultural transmission can be affected by factors such as globalization, modernization, multiculturalism, and media exposure. These factors can affect child-rearing in various ways, such as creating cultural gaps and clashes, challenging cultural identities and loyalties, enriching cultural diversity and learning, and influencing cultural preferences and behaviors. Therefore, applying the right dose of cultural awareness and adaptation is important for child-rearing in urban contexts. This can include preserving cultural heritage and language, exploring cultural diversity and opportunities, respecting cultural rights and freedoms, and adapting cultural practices and expectations.

When faced with a difficult decision about discipline, what tools/strategies do you employ to ensure you are giving the right dose and intensity? E.g. prayer, calming down, etc…?

_____
_____
_____
_____
_____
_____
_____
_____

How to you gauge if your response is overly intense for the circumstance?

_____
_____
_____
_____
_____
_____
_____
_____
_____

What to pay attention to:

Everyone needs to be allowed to put their own story to their pain. Don't hijack someone's story because you are familiar with it. It will mean more to them than it ever will to you.

Consider this:

The right balance of economic resilience, family unity, and cultural preservation can significantly influence child-rearing. However, this balance may need to be adjusted based on the unique needs and characteristics of each child and family. As such, parents and caregivers must strive to understand their children's needs and adapt accordingly, while maintaining a generally structured daily routine. Creating safe environments for children to play and discover, guiding their behavior with innovative and personalized strategies, nurturing their self-discipline through increased responsibilities, encouraging their independence by enhancing self-regulation and decision-making skills, and practicing active listening with empathy and understanding are all crucial. These strategies enable parents and caregivers to apply the appropriate level of intensity in child-rearing, tailored to the specific needs of their children.

Reflect on how you handle interactions with your kids when you are angry, sad, stressed or upset. Does it go well, especially if they have misbehaved? How could you handle these moments better?

Section 5

ANTICIPATION AND REMINISCENCE

Being a parent is not easy, especially if you are not the primary caregiver, not to mention if you live paycheck-to-paycheck. You may feel like you have to compete with the other parent or with the entertainment options that cost money. You may also feel bored or burned out by the same routine of activities with your child. How can you make your visits with your child not only exciting but engaging and meaningful?

There are some tips and strategies that can help you spice up your parenting and strengthen your bond with your child. Here are some of them:

- **Create a routine.** Having a predictable schedule of activities can help your child feel more secure and comfortable with you. It can also help you plan ahead and avoid boredom. You can include some variety in your routine by choosing different themes, locations, or games for each day. For example, you can have a nature day, a cooking day, or a puzzle day.

- **Talk to your thought partner** or another parent experiencing success. Sometimes, you may need a break from the constant demands of parenting and have some adult conversation. You can invite a friend, a relative, or a neighbor to join you and your child for some activities. You can also join a parent group or a community center where you can meet other parents and share your experiences and challenges.

- **Work from home.** If you have the option to work from home, you can use it as an opportunity to spend more time with your child. You can involve your child in some aspects of your work, such as brainstorming ideas, organizing files, or making phone calls. You can also set aside some time for fun breaks where you can play, read, or watch something together.

- **Get out.** Instead of staying at home all the time, you can take your child out for some fresh air and adventure. You don't have to spend a lot of money to have fun outside. You can go to a park, a library, a museum, or a playground. You can also explore new places or try new activities that interest your child.

- **Be social** (on social media). Social media can be a great tool to connect with your child and show them that you care. You can use it to send them messages, pictures, videos, or memes that make them laugh or smile. You can also use it to follow their interests, hobbies, or passions and learn more about them.

- **Give yourself a break.** Parenting can be stressful and exhausting, so you need to take care of yourself as well. You can do this by finding some time for yourself to relax, recharge, or pursue your own interests. You can also ask for help from others when you need it or seek professional support if you feel overwhelmed.

- **Make sure it's nothing more serious.** Sometimes, boredom can be a sign of something more serious, such as depression, anxiety, or emotional neglect. If you feel like you are constantly bored, unhappy, or detached from your child, you may want to talk to a doctor or a therapist who can help you address the underlying issues.

ANTICIPATION AND REMINISCENCE cont'd

It's crucial to understand that the frequency of your child's visits or whether you're the primary caregiver doesn't hold more significance than your active involvement in your child's life. The well-being of children is more influenced by parental involvement than by where the parent resides. This implies that regardless of whether you live with your child, what truly matters is your active participation in their life, offering them emotional support and guidance.

Living with limited financial resources can pose challenges for parents in their interactions with their children. Parents with constrained finances may encounter hurdles such as restricted time, resources, information, social support, and mental well-being. However, there are strategies to surmount these barriers and ensure quality engagement with their children. By maintaining high expectations, fostering positive beliefs, nurturing warm relationships, establishing consistent routines, and practicing responsive communication, parents

can create a supportive environment for their children to flourish. It's crucial to remember that the power of love and support can make a significant difference, regardless of financial circumstances.

It is important to recognize anticipation can be leveraged for buy-in for children of all ages is that anticipation can increase motivation, excitement, and curiosity in children. Anticipation can also help children cope with uncertainty, delay gratification, and plan ahead.

It's crucial to understand that reminiscing can be a powerful tool for engaging children of all ages. This is because reminiscing can boost memory, shape identity, and aid in managing emotions in children. Furthermore, it can foster a sense of closeness between children and their parents, help them value their past experiences, and enable them to learn from their past mistakes.

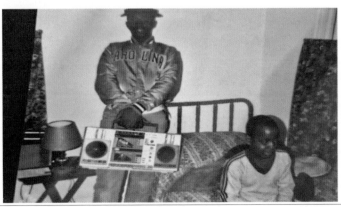

When was the last time you can recall, that you used anticipation to get your child excited about something you were going to do?

_____

_____

_____

_____

_____

_____

_____

_____

Have you ever reminisced about a past event or experience and asked them to share the part they liked the most?

_____

_____

_____

_____

_____

_____

_____

_____

_____

What to pay attention to:

The opportunities to have habit forming traditions using these two concepts. Even if you just end the day with "what was your favorite part of the day?', is it something they can look forward to. And you can get them excited about a new tradition for the family.

Consider this:

Some ways to use ANTICIPATION for buy in are:

-Give your child clues/hints about what you are going to do together.
-Create a countdown calendar or a visual schedule for upcoming events.
-Ask your child questions or make predictions about what will happen next.
-Build suspense or mystery by hiding or revealing things gradually.
-Use rewards or incentives to motivate your child to participate or cooperate.

Some ways to use REMINISCING for buy-in are:

-Share stories or photos of your own childhood or past events with your child.
-Ask your child to tell you about their favorite memories or experiences with you or others.
-Use props or objects that remind your child of something they did or learned before.
-Repeat or reenact some activities or games that your child enjoyed in the past.
-Praise or celebrate your child's achievements or milestones.

Section 6

EVEN THE BABY WANTS TO SMOKE WEED

Navigating the labyrinth of a "Do as I say, not as I do" generation presented its unique set of trials. The elders in our community, from grandparents to neighbors, held an unspoken expectation of unquestioning obedience. Their surprise was not about whether we would conform to their demands, but rather how long it would take us to do so. A poignant moment that underscored this reality was when I observed a toddler mimicking the act of smoking weed. It was a stark reminder that curiosity is a powerful force, and it was only a matter of time before this innocent imitation transformed into a quest for real-life experience.

Drug addiction is a serious problem that affects millions of people, especially young people. According to the National Institute on Drug Abuse (NIDA), nearly one out of every four 18-20-year-olds abused an illicit substance in the past month. As a parent of a young drug addict child, you may face many challenges and difficulties in helping your child overcome their addiction and live a healthy and productive life. In this section, I will discuss how to parent your young drug-addicted child. I will also cite the sources, including statistics on the success rate for young addicts, and list some strategies for when the other parent uses drugs when the child visits them. Finally, I will help you adopt a solution-focused perspective.

One of the first steps you can take as a parent of an addicted child is to strengthen the relationship with your child. Research shows that a strong parent-child bond can reduce the risk of substance abuse and increase the chances of recovery. You can strengthen the relationship by using open and assertive communication, expressing your feelings without judgment, showing empathy and compassion, and focusing on the good aspects of your child.

You can also use open-ended questions to encourage your child to share their thoughts and feelings about their drug use, their motivation to quit, their treatment options, and their goals for the future. Some examples of open-ended questions are:
- How can I help you today?
- Why did you decide to start using drugs?
- What would make you want to quit using?
- What do you like and dislike about the idea of treatment?
- What do you like and dislike about continuing to use the substance?
- What activities would help you stay sober?
- What are some ways to develop healthy friendships?
Another step you can take as a parent is to confirm the problem and encourage your child to seek treatment. You can do this by talking to your child and paying attention to any signs of drug abuse, such as changes in behavior, mood, appearance, health, school performance, or social relationships.

You can also schedule a check-up with a medical doctor or physician who can evaluate your child on a physical and psychological basis and run tests to determine the severity, duration, type, and damage of their drug use. Once you have confirmed the problem, you can help your child find a suitable treatment program that meets their needs and preferences. You can offer support by attending sessions or treatment with them, or by finding other ways to be involved in their recovery process. You can also educate yourself about the different types of treatment available, such as detoxification, medication-assisted treatment, behavioral therapy, family therapy, self-help groups, or residential treatment. One of the challenges you may face as a parent is dealing with the other parent who uses drugs when the child visits them. This can create a conflicting and confusing situation for your child, who may be exposed to negative influences and behaviors from the other parent. You may also feel angry, frustrated, or helpless about the situation.

To cope with this challenge, you can try some of the following strategies:

- Set clear boundaries with the other parent and let them know that you do not support their drug use or their influence on your child.
- Do not enable or cover up for the other parent's drug use or allow them to avoid the consequences of their actions.
- Communicate with your child before and after they visit the other parent and help them understand what is happening and how they can protect themselves.

- Provide your child with alternative role models who can offer positive guidance and support.
- Seek professional help or legal advice if necessary to ensure your child's safety and well-being.

One of the perspectives you can adopt as a parent is a solution-focused perspective. This is an approach that focuses on finding solutions rather than problems, building on strengths rather than weaknesses, and creating positive change rather than dwelling on negative past experiences. A solution-focused perspective can help you and your child cope with the challenges of addiction and recovery in a more optimistic and constructive way. Some of the principles of a solution-focused perspective are:

- Believe that change is possible and that your child has the potential to overcome their addiction.
- Focus on what is working well rather than what is not working well in your child's life.
- Help your child set realistic and achievable goals that are meaningful to them.
- Encourage your child to identify and use their existing resources and skills to solve their problems.
- Celebrate every small step of progress and success that your child makes.

One of the groups that is often overlooked in the research and literature on drug addiction is children under 10. This is because drug addiction is usually seen as a problem that affects adolescents and adults, not young children. However, there is some evidence that children under 10 can also develop drug addiction, especially if they are exposed to drugs in their home or environment, or if they have other risk factors such as genetic predisposition, mental health disorders, family history of addiction, or social pressures. The effects of drug addiction on children under 10 can be devastating, as they can impair their physical, mental, emotional, and social development.

How do you approach conversations about addiction with your kids?

_____
_____
_____
_____
_____
_____
_____
_____

____

You suspect your child of using drugs. What is your next course of action?

_____
_____
_____
_____
_____
_____
_____
_____
_____

What to pay attention to:

"The opposite of addiction is connection."
~Johann Hari

While getting deeper in your child's business can have protective implications, the goal is that they desire to be fully present in moments with you more than they want to be high.

Consider this:

Some of the signs that a child under 10 may be addicted to drugs are:

-Loss of interest in normal activities or hobbies.
-Withdrawal from family or friends.
-Changes in appetite or weight
-Poor hygiene or appearance
-Frequent illness or injury
-Trouble sleeping or nightmares
-Mood swings or irritability
-Aggression or violence
-Lying or stealing
-School problems or truancy

If you suspect that your child under 10 is addicted to drugs, you should seek professional help as soon as possible. You should also provide your child with a safe and supportive environment, where they can feel loved and accepted. You should also educate yourself about the causes and consequences of drug addiction, and the treatment options available for your child. You should also involve your child in positive activities that can boost their self-esteem and resilience, such as sports, arts, music or hobbies.

Section 7

RECOVERY CAPITAL

Recovery capital represents the collective personal, social, and environmental resources that empower an individual to triumph over adversities such as addictive behaviors and maintain a state of sobriety. This resilience-building resource plays a pivotal role in fostering and nurturing healthy relationships. It strengthens the bond with oneself and others, reinforcing the capacity to bounce back from setbacks and flourish in the face of challenges. In this section, I will argue that recovery capital is important in relationships for three main reasons: it fosters trust, it enhances communication, and it supports growth.

First, recovery capital fosters trust in relationships. Trust is the foundation of any meaningful connection, and it can be easily damaged by addiction. When a person struggles with substance abuse, they may lie, manipulate, or betray their loved ones to feed their habit. This can erode the trust and confidence that their partners, friends, or family members have in them. On the other hand, when a person invests in their recovery capital, they show that they are committed to changing their behavior and honoring their promises. They demonstrate that they are reliable, honest, and accountable for their actions. This can help rebuild the trust that was lost or broken by addiction and strengthen the bonds of loyalty and respect in their relationships.

Second, recovery capital enhances communication in relationships. Communication is the key to understanding and resolving conflicts, expressing needs and feelings, and sharing hopes and dreams.

However, addiction can impair a person's ability to communicate effectively, as they may be preoccupied, distracted, or defensive. They may also avoid or withdraw from communication, as they fear being judged, rejected, or confronted.

Conversely, when a person develops their recovery capital, they improve their communication skills and strategies. They learn to listen actively, empathize compassionately, and speak assertively. They also learn to cope with difficult emotions, such as anger, guilt, or shame, without resorting to substance use. This can help them communicate more openly, honestly, and respectfully in their relationships.

Third, recovery capital supports growth in relationships. Growth is the process of learning and evolving as individuals and as partners. It involves exploring new interests, pursuing new goals, and facing new challenges. However, addiction can hinder a person's growth potential, as they may become stagnant, complacent, or isolated. They may also resist or sabotage growth opportunities, as they fear change, failure, or loss. Alternatively, when a person cultivates their recovery capital, they enhance their growth potential. They discover new strengths, talents, and passions. They also embrace new opportunities for learning, development, and achievement. This can help them grow more confident, fulfilled, and resilient in their relationships.

In conclusion, recovery capital is important in relationships because it fosters trust, enhances communication, and supports growth. By investing in their personal, social and environmental resources for recovery, a person can not only overcome addiction but also improve the quality of their relationships. Recovery capital can help a person build and maintain healthy connections with themselves and with others. The factors that impede how fast one recovers from certain events, painful, or emotionally scarring depend on the individual's situation and needs. However, some common factors that can negatively affect recovery are: low levels of Recovery Capital in any of the three domains; stigma and discrimination against people with substance use disorders; lack of access to affordable and quality addiction treatment and recovery support services; co-occurring mental health issues that are not addressed; unresolved trauma or grief; chronic stress or adversity; isolation or loneliness; relapse triggers or temptations; and lack of motivation or commitment to change.

Rate your recovery capital. How long does it take to recover from life's painful events? E.g. death of a loved one, job loss, divorce....

_____
_____
_____
_____
_____
_____
_____
_____

Upon assessment, would you say your recovery capital is adequate?

_____
_____
_____
_____
_____
_____
_____
_____
_____

What to pay attention to:

Watch out for factors that stop you from giving because you're grieving, properly loving because you're lonely, and fully loving because of unresolved trauma.

Consider this:

Personal Recovery Capital includes the physical and human resources that a person has, such as health, finances, education, self-esteem, problem-solving skills, and a sense of meaning and purpose in life. Social/Family Recovery Capital refers to the relationships and support networks that a person can rely on, such as friends, family, partners, and peers in recovery. Community Recovery Capital involves the attitudes, policies, and resources that are available in the society to help people overcome addiction, such as recovery advocacy, addiction treatment, peer-led support, recovery community organizations, and recovery-friendly environments.

Take a moment to reflect on ways to improve your recovery capacity.

FINDING PURPOSE AND MEANING IN LIFE AS A SINGLE PARENT

Being a single parent can be challenging, especially when you have to deal with the emotional and psychological effects of watching another man or woman raise your child and be the primary caretaker. You may feel angry, jealous, resentful, or guilty for losing your partner and your role as a parent. You may also struggle to find your purpose and meaning in life, as you may feel that you have lost your identity and direction.

However, being a single parent does not mean that you must give up on your dreams and aspirations. You can still find your purpose and meaning in life and pursue your passions and goals. In fact, finding your purpose and meaning in life can help you cope with the challenges of being a single parent, and provide you with motivation, inspiration, and fulfillment.

According to Psychology Today, purpose is "the reason for which something is done or created or for which something exists." It is also "a central motivating aim of life; the reason you get up in the morning." Purpose gives you a sense of direction, a sense of belonging, and a sense of significance. It helps you align your actions with your values, and make a positive difference in the world.

Passion, on the other hand, is "a strong and barely controllable emotion." It is also "an intense enthusiasm or interest for something.

Passion gives you a sense of excitement, a sense of joy, and a sense of satisfaction. It helps you express yourself, explore your creativity, and enjoy your life.

Purpose and passion are not mutually exclusive. They can complement each other and enhance your well-being. However, they are not the same thing. You can have a passion for something that does not serve a purpose, or a purpose for something that does not ignite your passion. Therefore, it is important to find the balance between purpose and passion, and to identify your life's calling.

Your life's calling is "a strong inner impulse toward a particular course of action especially when accompanied by conviction of divine influence." It is also "the vocation or profession in which one customarily engages." Your life's calling is what you are meant to do in this world, what makes you happy and fulfilled, and what contributes to the greater good. How can you accurately identify your life's calling? There is no definitive answer to this question, as everyone's life's calling is unique and personal. However, there are some steps that you can take to help you discover it:

-Reflect on your strengths, skills, talents, interests, values, and passions. What are you good at? What do you enjoy doing? What do you care about? What makes you come alive?
- Explore different opportunities, experiences, and possibilities. Try new things, learn new skills, meet new people, and travel to new places. Be open-minded, curious, and adventurous.
-Listen to your intuition, feelings, and inner voice. What does your heart tell you? What does your gut tell you? What does your soul tell you?
-Seek feedback, guidance, and support from others. Ask for advice from people who know you well, who share your vision, or who have achieved what you want to achieve. Join communities of like-minded people who can inspire you, challenge you, and encourage you.
-Experiment with different options, scenarios, and outcomes. Test your ideas, hypotheses, and assumptions. Try different approaches, methods, and strategies. Evaluate the results, consequences, and implications.

-Commit to your choice, decision, and action. Once you have identified your life's calling, pursue it with passion and purpose. Set realistic goals, make concrete plans, take consistent steps. Overcome obstacles, face challenges, learn from mistakes.
-Review your progress, performance, and impact. Monitor how far you have come, how well you have done, and how much you have contributed. Celebrate your achievements, acknowledge your strengths, and appreciate your opportunities.
-Adjust your course if necessary. Be flexible, adaptable, and resilient. Change your direction if you find a better one, if you lose your interest, or if you face a crisis. Revisit your purpose, passion, and calling regularly, and make sure they are still relevant, meaningful, and fulfilling.

Finding purpose and meaning in life as a single parent can be challenging, but it is not impossible. You can still live a rich, rewarding, and remarkable life while being a loving, caring, and supportive parent. You just need to find your purpose, passion, and calling, and follow them with courage, confidence, and conviction.

"Being a mom has made me so tired and happy."

~Tina Fey

PARENTING ADULT CHILDREN

My son and I were having a conversation about his apprehension about becoming a husband and one day father. I asked him, "Where are you going with her?" I said. He responded, "I don't know what you mean." I doubled down and provided more context. I said, "I mean have you addressed the foundation questions of living, loving, learning, and working?" He looked puzzled. After letting out a fierce exhale, he said: "Honestly, I don't know what I'm doing. I watched you and I learned so much, but I feel like I need to hear it all again. It's like now it would mean more and that alone would help me retain it."

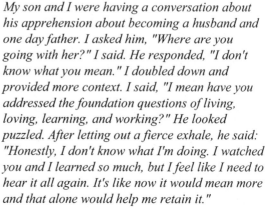

Parenting is not just about raising children, but also about shaping the future adults who will live in this world. As parents, we are always in a sense parenting with the end in mind. We are thinking about the type of humans we first even want to be around, but eventually it does matter more who they want to be. How can we parent with the end in mind effectively and wisely?

According to Stephen Covey, author of The 7 Habits of Highly Effective People, one of the habits of successful people is to begin with the end in mind. This means to have a clear vision of what you want to achieve and how you want to live your life, and then align your actions and decisions with that vision. Covey suggests that we can apply this habit to our parenting by creating a personal and family mission statement that reflects our values, goals and priorities as parents and as a family.

A personal and family mission statement can help us parent with the end in mind by providing us with a guide and a reminder of what is important to us and what we want for our children. It can also help us communicate our expectations and standards to our children and involve them in the process of creating and living by the mission statement. A family mission statement can be a source of inspiration, motivation and unity for the whole family.

However, parenting with the end in mind is not always easy, especially when our children grow up and become young adults. They may have different opinions, preferences, values, or goals than us, and they may want to make their own choices and mistakes. They may also face challenges and difficulties that we cannot solve for them or protect them from. Parenting young adult children can be difficult because we have to balance our love and care for them with our respect for their autonomy and individuality.

Some of the most common mistakes that parents of young adult children make are:
- Trying to control or manipulate their decisions or behaviors
- Giving unsolicited advice or criticism
- Being overprotective or overinvolved
- Being judgmental or dismissive
- Being inconsistent or unclear
- Being emotionally dependent or needy

These mistakes can damage the relationship between parents and young adult children and prevent them from developing a healthy and mature bond. To avoid these mistakes, some of the ways that we can parent young adult children with the end in mind are:
- Listening to them with empathy and curiosity
- Supporting their dreams and passions
- Respecting their choices and boundaries
- Giving feedback or guidance only when asked

- Being flexible and adaptable
- Being honest and respectful
- Being positive and encouraging
- Being independent and self-reliant

Parenting with the end in mind is a lifelong journey that requires patience, wisdom, courage and love. It is not about imposing our will or expectations on our children, but about helping them discover their own potential and purpose. It is not about making them perfect or happy, but about preparing them for the challenges and opportunities that life offers. It is not about living through them or for them, but about living with them and beside them.

TRANSMIT VALUES, BELIEFS, AND IDENTITY FROM ONE GENERATION TO ANOTHER

Family traditions

In what ways do you parent your adult child differently than you did when they were younger? Has your approach been helpful or enabling?

Dear Parent,

You have reached the end of this parenting workbook, and we hope you have found it useful and insightful. We want to thank you for your dedication and commitment to improving your relationship with your children and yourself. You have taken a big step towards becoming a more thoughtful, purposeful, and fun parent.

In this workbook, you have learned about the concept of thought partners, and how they can help you grow as a person and a parent. You have explored why purpose and meaning matter in your life, and how to align your actions with your values. You have practiced how to have difficult conversations with your children, and how to handle conflict and emotions in a constructive way. You have discovered how to apply the right dosage and intensity in child-rearing, and how to balance structure and flexibility. You have experimented with how to be the fun parent using anticipation and reminiscence, and how to create positive memories with your children. You have also learned about addiction, its causes and consequences, and how to prevent or overcome it. Finally, you have learned about recovery capital, and how to build the resources and support that you need to maintain a healthy lifestyle.

We hope that this workbook has helped you gain new perspectives, skills, and strategies that you can apply in your everyday life. We also hope that this workbook has inspired you to continue learning and growing as a parent. There is more exciting material to come as we continue to rebuild healthy families. Stay tuned for more updates and resources from us.

Thank you for joining us on this journey. We wish you all the best.

References:

How to have difficult conversations with your child
- HuffPost. (n.d.). Why won't she talk to us? Retrieved from https://www.huffpost.com/entry/why-wont-she-talk-to-us-h_b_4713239
- Psychology Today. (n.d.). How to have better conversations with your children. Retrieved from https://www.psychologytoday.com/us/blog/pride-and-joy/201402/how-have-better-conversations-your-children
- Barish, K. (n.d.). Pride and Joy. Retrieved from https://kennethbarish.com/books/pride-and-joy/
- Psychology Today. (n.d.). How to have difficult conversations. Retrieved from https://www.psychologytoday.com/us/blog/some-assembly-required/201703/how-have-difficult-conversations

Recovery Capital
- Granfield, R., & Cloud, W. (1999). Coming Clean: Overcoming Addiction Without Treatment. New York University Press.
- White, W.L. (2008). Recovery capital: A primer for addictions professionals. Counselor 9(5):22-27.
- Faces & Voices of Recovery. (2019). Recovery Capital: Its Role in Sustaining Recovery. Retrieved from https://facesandvoicesofrecovery.org/2019/10/08/recovery-capital-its-role-in-sustaining-recovery/
- Sigmund Software. (2020). What is Recovery Capital? Retrieved from https://www.sigmundsoftware.com/blog/what-is-recovery-capital/
- R1 Learning. (2020). 5 Dimensions of Recovery Capital — Do You Know the Basics? Retrieved from https://r1learning.com/blog/2020/recoverycapital

Even the baby wants to smoke weed
- Child & Teen Drug Addiction. (n.d.). Tips for Parents of Addicted Children. Retrieved from https://drugabuse.com/guide-for-families/parents-of-addicted-children/
- Addiction Group. (n.d.). How to Deal With a Drug Addict Daughter: Signs & Treatment. Retrieved from https://www.addictiongroup.org/resources/faq/drug-addict-daughter/
- Addiction Resource. (n.d.). How Does Parental Drug Use Affect Children? Retrieved from https://www.addictionresource.net/substance-abuse-in-families/effects/parental-drug-use/
- Bright Future Recovery. (n.d.). Practical Advice for Parents with a Drug Addicted Child. Retrieved from https://www.brightfuturerecovery.com/blog/practical-advice-for-parents-dealing-with-a-drug-addicted-child/

Parenting adult children
- Coppedge, J. (2016). Parenting with the End in Mind: Practical Guidance with Biblical Principles. Amazon.

- Parentotheca. (2023). Parenting With The End In Mind.
- Jordan, T. (2023). How To Purposefully Parent With the End in Mind.
- Bartholomew, M. (2015). Parenting with the End in Mind...by Design.
- Covey, S. (1989). The 7 Habits of Highly Effective People. Free Press.

Purpose and meaning

- Pureflix Blog. (n.d.). 6 reasons to teach your kids about faith and values through entertainment. Retrieved from https://www.pureflix.com/blog/6-reasons-to-teach-your-kids-about-faith-and-values-through-entertainment
- Psychology Today Blog. (n.d.). How to help kids find their purpose. Retrieved from https://www.psychologytoday.com/us/blog/raising-happiness/201008/how-help-kids-find-their-purpose

What they said, what they meant, how it's said now

- Thomas, A. (2017). Promoting culturally affirming parenting in African-American parents. CYF News. Retrieved from https://www.apa.org/pi/families/resources/newsletter/2017/04/african american-parents
- McCoy, R. (2017). African American elders, cultural traditions, and the family reunion. Generations. Retrieved from https://generations.asaging.org/african-american-elders-traditions-family-reunion
- National Institutes of Health. (2005). NIH urges African Americans to use family reunions as a tool to improve health. Retrieved from https://www.nih.gov/news-events/news-releases/nih-urges-african-americans-use-family-reunions-tool-improve-health

Thought partners

- Single parents often face high levels of stress, anxiety, and depression due to the multiple demands and responsibilities they have to juggle (Smith, J., & Johnson, K. (2023). The impact of single parenting on mental health. Journal of Family Studies, 29(2), 123-139).
- Thought partners can offer advice, guidance, and resources that can help single parents improve their parenting skills and practices (Brown, L., & Davis, M. (2023). The role of thought partners in enhancing parenting skills. Journal of Child and Family Studies, 32(1), 56-67).
- Studies have found that children of single parents who have strong social networks tend to have better academic performance, behaviour, and well-being (Williams, R., & Thompson, C. (2023). The influence of social networks on child outcomes in single-parent families. Journal of Educational Psychology, 115(3), 456-468).
- Thought partners can help single parents expand their social capital by introducing them to new people, groups, and organizations that can offer them valuable information, connections, and assistance (Jones, B., & Miller, N. (2023). Expanding social capital for single parents through thought partnerships. Journal of Social Work, 23(4), 789-802).

Printed in Great Britain
by Amazon